THE EXQUISITE BUOYANCIES

THE EXQUISITE BUOYANCIES

ASHLEY CHAMBERS

NEW MICHIGAN PRESS
TUCSON, ARIZONA

NEW MICHIGAN PRESS
DEPT OF ENGLISH, P. O. BOX 210067
UNIVERSITY OF ARIZONA
TUCSON, AZ 85721-0067

<http://newmichiganpress.com>

Orders and queries to <nmp@thediagram.com>.

ISBN 978-1-934832-80-6. FIRST PRINTING.

Design by Ander Monson.

Cover art by Arrington de Dionyso.

CONTENTS

for le rata

Behind God's eyes
There might
Be other lights

Mina Loy

Very Sore & So Asunder commune in a braided fingerhastening to fasten
my riddleroused incantation   So Awake   I cannot keep busy any longer
w the tremendous double
-jointed Truth —

Here is this echo
Terrible Here
is this echo
I make
alone
Alone

& Here in my hands Here
unstrapped
1 flaccidlipped linnet coughing up clandestine
forktender factualities
lest Terrible echoes
again —

Baby You   You Little
Echo
Again —

& again w 1 heisted hen
cipherclenched cluckwise
between
my bosomless forlorn
my own extant maternalwillies
gone goosely savage
yr acrobatic eensy jeebies
our scrupling

sepulcher pliant —

I begin,

Baby, by treading unlit dust w my
Instruments of Enamel
& inquiring
if You can
forge me some Old Light
if You can *Be Light* Named Old I beseech
yr body back because Baby *You are*
Light Appeared

& doubling 1 richly colored Exalt toward yr body-body —

Baby You,
a precede fruit spreading seedless turbulence, a stiffening
of lips flattening my already-yield w mistless language-Mercy,

A leashed Lightmouth leading me to White Kneel—

This Crafted

Left To Itself

on knees So Awake reappearing

when & then once more

on uprightest knell wrecked w wailing

wren —

Passerine or person I bid them now
to pant or perch a plural
Blessed Event peeping Also Born
from my lukewarm
mamamind stretched down
-right noisome
-sough, a supersession of Yr Long Since,
You Little
Please Do Not Depart

in Knockless Know —

Yes   Honey   You

a sprawling skyline stanzic unescorted

a recumbent cadence now absorbed in mother's fingerfeel —

Little Little Ripest Exile   Moonwalking Whitest White   Guide All
The Tongue-Tied Angels Baby   to mama's
Trumped Up Empyrean
Glockenspiel —

Vertical the bornest talk yr bleated bearer pinkied into posture   & Echo
Baby, Bringeth echo
Echo me back into consecrated
place
to play in placeless hallow rosy

Where —

Awake's Agape   rustles a little   or a little recess   recesses bright
You Little Recess Bright   upon which shores   You Little
Skein of Drawers   avalanching widest 1st for Whose Ashamed
to hesitate   my Disbanded
Soft Soft Stances summoning   yr 1 & only
face —

Frocked in The Hereafter,
A deep & weep
-ing lustrous
You Little
Summon Face taking sudden seraphic sail
You Little Breezy Freak
of Fractured Face —

Babbling on behalf
of Whose doubly-   beaked Jitterfauna for aye
disgraced w a woozyhead

-ed finesse unlike my counterfeit vapid rabbits lamenting
Familiar What in sissy gulps so very wince
& wry w nothing short of
Sure, Here's

1 more senile
Ploverwhy
duckwading away in silent   worrywobble from   My

Insane Assay At Acquisition My faltering seize
because not You baby
not
You —

My Little Babbler must be
Seamless Large & eyeing The Chatterless
Tremors among us
dropping
stars
as if
to compensate
for my now weightless freight in Whose Backlit Alone & to what degree
or for what price or w my own
White Creature Hands —

Groping wide for surplus syllables
summoning the 1 & only face
Syllables To Summon Yr Little Face
in the Moldering Outgrown
a dark-windowed peninsula of nauseous shames
The nameless
of yr
Roughly Organs just about became The Bringeth
of softest stances echo wide
Bringeth echo —

Echo to illuminate   The Holy Sick   in my own vanish

Echo I
illuminate my Honest
& my Honest professes I am 1 of The Little Babble
r's loosed   stars
sounding ill
cold violet sobs puzzlepieced
or plucked nighestnigh from
You
will   never   be
a   body   I can hold or feed —

So call me a Very Milky Woman then
to pour you now from my cries
I course until I'm streaming

material light —

You issue forth

but this time I am instead drowning An entire unabridged lordylegion
of lousylunged linnets

their crimson foreheads begging to be
Another of my bogus
beginnings
pressurized & then smashed against

Song

the size of 1 rock —

Songest Rock, now w my chirrups swollen in shriekiest tenor manifold —

You Little Soddy Sod All Flock To Really Freak My Flocky Freak Yes 1 Talismanic Apparition Pigtailed Shrewd in Splinterswerve Behold, Songrock, I croon to unsteady & salute my stalactitic daggerloon to loony

loon —

Baby You
bend above
me
in obviated white
-est white
susceptible to Song
-est Rock I tantrum
-trill rockyfine

a solemn
Song —

1 sympathetic light slipsearching in secret ache for white
my fingers long & under yr weather Baby You white the white   the

White —

Needles to say I'm still cloudy around the gills
for My Little Firmamental Bright —

You Little
Glistered Tonguenuzzle Therefroming in Whose
Discerning Sky
-larked Parade of Sweet

until my Soonest shilly-shalls
The Already Indwelled Nevermore
of our 1 pooled
& foolishpooling face —

The beclouded
squawking Savant

Soul Thrown Back

The beclouded
espied to refrain from

onto the lands x 2

The beclouded songstress
What
no Figmented

could ever cowslip
to here again want —

Okay but already having Partaken in yr partookenest lickety-split

Oh Baby

You learned

asteroids,

a legless erect amid reverent results —

The unsurrendering

tune of my regret

a paralytic fog —

& then what but A tongue A tongue Yr firmamental tonguing
of my bedimmed saddest shook,
yr broken down body-body
in 2-faced measure unskied I did

w my 1st & deadliest
thin-skinned look —

Baby, this linnet
is half-rabbit

A Creepy Climber of yr Risen Freckled A Snivel Toiler w toothy starlit
for dialect dizzying
1 axiom seldom warmer
& yet ayonder eclipsed

in Whose Ascurry but a soul —

yr body-body ascample —

In The Fluent Overcast   I gutbeam to incarnate each dawning descent,
tailless & testament   to Whose Role   but The Ploverwhy Still Pleading
for my tight-lipped taciturn of fangydark   where linnetlambs loaf
in idlesprawl   in naked unaware   weighed in Whose Greedygrout
or breathygod enough   to sanctuaryswine my tenderwrath so massacre
I'm syllabicating until the cows come home a Honey Baby Goreabout —

In breathless bodice see
I also bagged this Baby
or this linnet
is not You, Baby

because tussock too severe for swaddling
Die Once lives the Endeared
Beyond & twice betokens each ethereal blow

I suit up to bliss out
Yr kingdom of Wingless Multitude mooring murderous for my

mammary drought —

In my brains or yr brains,
Baby
The same brains Baby

This linnet
is neither You nor rabbit

but somewhere, Honey, I stroke his Long Furless
Doughy Ears

until my hands slow down for the *Let Go* —

The *Let Go* somewhere, Baby,

Somewhere Honey,
You
better call me
a Very Milky
Woman because I was once
yr mother —

You Little Affright Asleep Breathless & Never In Repose
You Little Knife To Stir My Cobwebs To Their Feet
You Little Werehere Once But Then Distantdead in My Loneliestbelow
You Little Never Ever Losing Luster You
You Little Amaranthed Asunder Who
unhanding celestial as you do
You Little Throning Above in Towering Sense of Airsick Sedate
avowing audacious astral until my own heedless rocking supple elucidates
a drove of the Widest-Wandering Ogled-Blown I Alight
my sickly imagination thus having stirred this gaggle's phantom pinion
to its palest eviscerated plight —

Maybe baby, You,   maybe if You could be the one to name me

strip Song bare
w yr Companion Voice   constructed   from   *Make clear*

my naked muzzle was
                    Yr Aching Along   You Little Fox   You Little

     Hybrid Sideways in Humansuit of Words —

Both of us smiling & laughing on land to keep my head warm & talking & normal   -looking   but No not w out You Honey do I have 1 face nor stomach   to host

what I am sorriest for in my Middle Thick —

& so w feeblest fire cadence I baptize my own drossy wormless my single-
handed devastating rapt,   my skull coronated in sputter to moan

1

Piousgowned Apt —

My stupid burden of barren numb crowing
& cawing

to simper-seize the Where & Why of Mesmericly What
or Whose

Whose Creatures Deeply Unfiddled know for certain I am
the companionless matriarch of deadest smithereens slaught

& disemboweling even now shoulds Little Fox My Sweet Fox heaven

-ing to chirp in linnetlaced laugh —

1 sanguinary snarl of Who is

Hallowed Correctly to Caw

but the bellowed mew of howling just yet —

Baby blazing   in meteoritemute   in 1 Unachieved Know   You Little
Industrious Forgiven Beget —

Apply yr rapid half-rabbit nirvanasick
to my hemisphereless misery,

Yr almy perish to my sonic glossary,
Yr thee to my unheardest nothingelse,

Make some paradise of my tenterhookly unspokensofts or Prithee

Becometh the whole crawling galaxy

before I billow another moronic breeze
tending to the lowest common denominator of Cosmic Seems —

I'm Not Kidding You 1 Unpossessed Spangle of Psalmody,   upright that

Be
for me

You Little   Unending Procession of Soundless Company,
vertical that unrivaled qualmish
of yr unreachably caravanning honey —

Because I'm carpentering Honest ashore to footed-God Gold & Shalling my bent body until I am   1 lonesome bone   buoyant & holy fire better-fired for wordbearing You a second time —

You Baby Born —

This uneaten everlasting silk is yr skin & my milk songs ecstatic white
Hands Who Burn to contract yr death is now a story

I can report

w my Gold —

Little little Here here Little hither Here little
hangs
my trunked habit of 1 halted Gold
spilling yr crested Shall —

Little touch w out looking   Baby
touch

w out breathing   another deflated decoy

boohoo
-ing, a retarded
lamb mooing wildwide   eweless & baaless for body-body

but not You

baby   still not You —

Little Just just 1 more sputtering snare but not you baby until I sun
-silence my own cackle my own cluck or the Die Oftener until I white-
light What

I won't w out yr Secretswept Sacrament of the not Earth scarce
-ly advising a Fatalspeeching a Foundbeneather a Phonyluminous to stun
-bright You baby prostrating my benumbed oncepink,
the plush
cradle white but ascending still for Who but
You Born
to consume the Event Born
again if only
to depart again

No, Live not into an Again but

A Live, You Little

Vindicated Ruddy Adroit
Live

Baby, Live —

Live my reorganize of seed   & some other angels maybe   The Unvoiced
  If Ever God forbade me to render in perennial bloods

Yes   Little   Manifest   Martian   my manifest bloods ravenous
bloods w voice ajar yes & the bulk the bulk
                    of yr body-body   also song
are the white parts mating still —

A climb of grief I weep-wade to examine yr gums laid bare like blessing
in gorgeous permission my Alien Power embers yr soft skull

in Unthreatening Gesture
in placement of Celestial Diadem
in Loud Snap

You are the More Song

You White Little Fox —

The white parts echo again the white parts to make me crazy the white parts who go running the white parts keeping busy w the tremendous white parts Who Rise Up against the white parts I bury yr nose the cocoon white your mouth white & awash w white I iron yr brows against the white piers echo again I press yr wet mouth into my white wet palm yr tongue floundering to snake against the white parts yr tongue against my white wet palm goes running makes me crazy the white cradle running to make me crazy the white parts mating weep-wading to examine my blessing My Baby You Gorgeous My Alien White My Alien Parts go running You go running You must go running Baby you must —

Baby I behold you somewhere doing that fugitive Purple
Cloud

& the Robe you wear is slaughtered from our shared skin —

Yr softshaven noodlenut weeping for milk I cannot grow
weary w pinched fingers firm enough & my milk

meek, teat zilch to beckon my own doubtless
pathetic milk dim
& dosing
in departed synonym —

my milk
my milk
my milk
is dead now too died when You died Honey —

Yr mother is yr illest star pendulous & casting into

the wide Earth

again & again & again a black boneless cow —

Baby I am the sorriest I have ever been I am 2 women
at the same
time falling down
to weep together w out You
My Bosomless Birdbrained
Dopey Lame

w out You carrying colorless slaught nowhere w out You

I am paltry cow w Very Song
Baaaaaaaaaaaaaaaa

who knee-tarries & shakes & shakes to shook out No Other Prayer Left
Here to sow belted against bold but blistered airs except maybe baby

please inside yr Skywide Cavernous Ears yr Perfect Weightless

Nauseous Spellbound my *Let Go* mating echoes feralsigh
& you
answering my mournfilled nil to multiply

yr very own private High Up Violet Looks —

Little Little Swinging from Bravest Bare
My Honest says *You* & Not

Silk story-free
Here Gold speaks easy
to a Listen Low w Headless Heed

above this Earth laid pearly white where Light should look
like this —

Light

should roll & rise & stand Upright w out Recur,

& Light should look

only once —

& The Should should not look back to I
illuminate   the sick in any vanish not mine not yrs
or to any body-body
back not ever Light should produce before perform —

all but eternal rest thrown back
like bats drinking straight from our veins
My Gorgeous Little Fox
Yr Fur So Soft
So Soft
My Walls So Moist
Growing Greenest Moss
Us so soft so moist You & Me laid down in linnetmoss
So that we both must rest & love each other even nearer than
The Before when I had never even met you yet —

Yes Here here inside Light   You claim as Place   abyss-incised
& image
        -free you are
                    Bloodlet a nerveless loose   into Incantation
So Awake you echo

now w out my help

            to utter in yr own Dart About —

You crazy wet
sapphire & 1 twisted knee Baby Honey Baby dashed & clambered
full-length into What
Is View

All Eyes Are Now Upon You

like *Look*
thus named *Light*
like *Linnet* who laughs laborious in warblelow delight —

You Little Let Light

You Let Light

Light

is the echo

again

Light

Echo again —

You Alien   to Alien We Sing   yes honey yr very own
    -ing

which ember soft laid skull but not to bury   bare   A See & casting-casting wide 1 Earth
    Who also   now
    unstories Light

    & Light Itself
    thus named

    Free —

ACKNOWLEDGMENTS

Thank you to Ander Monson and the editors at New Michigan Press for selecting my manuscript.

I'd also like to thank the following publications in which parts of this manuscript first appeared: *Prelude Magazine, Salt Hill Journal, Pinch Journal, Bone Bouquet, Sonora Review, 4ink7,* and *Omniverse.*

Thank you to sonic sorcerer and artist Arrington de Dionyso for divining the cover of this book.

The Exquisite Buoyancies would not exist without the encouragement, insight, and tenderness of my Tuscaloosan cosmic family: Abraham Smith, Shaelyn Smith, Jenifer Park, P.J. Williams, Stephen Thomas, Candystore, Eric Karin, Sally Roundhouse, Emma Zip Furman, Katy Rossing, Kirby Johnson, and Krystin Gollihue. I love you.

Thank you also to mentors Heidi Lynn Staples, Kellie Wells, Michael Martone, Robin Behn, and Peter Streckfus, for listening and perceiving something of otherworldly worth.

Finally, deepest gratitude to my sibylline sisters, Heidi Lynn Gustafson and M0PA, both of whom provided me with critical spiritual guidance through my most challenging hours—you are the queens of my heart and my immortal confidants, always.

ASHLEY CHAMBERS is a writer, multimedia artist, theologian, and educator. She holds a Master of Sacred Theology and Master of Divinity from Union Theological Seminary at Columbia University and an MFA in Creative Writing from the University of Alabama. You can find her at ashleyelizabethchambers.com.

COLOPHON

Text is set in a digital version of Jenson, designed by Robert Slimbach in 1996, and based on the work of punchcutter, printer, and publisher Nicolas Jenson. The titles here are in Futura.

❁

NEW MICHIGAN PRESS, based in Tucson, Arizona, prints poetry and prose chapbooks, especially work that transcends traditional genre. Together with *DIAGRAM*, NMP sponsors a yearly chapbook competition.

DIAGRAM, a journal of text, art, and schematic, is published bimonthly at THEDIAGRAM.COM. Periodic print anthologies are available from the New Michigan Press at NEWMICHIGANPRESS.COM.

www.ingramcontent.com/pod-product-compliance
Lightning Source LLC
Chambersburg PA
CBHW080941040426
42444CB00015B/3394